Training 4 Newbies Commercial Real Estate Finance

Quick Training Program

by

Isaac Arellano
Senior Underwriter
Commercial and Corporate Finance Specialist

Copyright © 2018

Introduction

The Lending industry has been one of the motors that keep the US economy at its best. Today most Real Estate developments and individual projects are possible thanks to Lenders who actively participate in this industry.

The Commercial Real Estate Finance Quick Training Program is a great introduction for professionals looking to venture into this fascinating and profitable industry.

I took the time to select the most important concepts required to understand the basics of Commercial Real Estate Finance.

TABLE OF CONTENTS

Introduction

Table of Contents

Legal Disclaimer

Chapter 1   Commercial Real Estate.

Chapter 2. Different Types of Commercial Real Estate

Chapter 3. Clasification of Commercial Real Estate

Chapter 4. CRE Finance

Chapter 5. Commercial Real Estate Lenders.

Chapter 6. Basics of Credit rating .

Chapter 7 Pre-Qualifying CRE Loans.

Chapter 8 Appraisals and CRE valuation.

About the Author

LEGAL DISCLAIMER

Commercial Real Estate Finance: Training for newbies
Isaac Arellano – Senior Underwriter

© 2018 Isaac Arellano
All Rights Reserbed.

Isaac Arellano – Senior Underwriter
Contact Information
intelligentfv@gmail.com
www.underwritingcre.ml

ISBN: 9781983225376

Thank you for downloading a digital copy of my book. Please be aware that this copy is meant to be for personal used only. The partial or total reproduction of this material is prohibited even if you have no intent to profit out of the illegal reproduction of this work. Now that you have your own copy please encourage friends and family to get their own by visiting Amazon books where they can find other titles and Authors related to this topic.

The author has made every effort to ensure the accuracy of the information within this book was correct at time of publication. The author does not assume and hereby disclaims any liability to any party for any loss, damage, or disruption caused by errors or omissions, whether such errors or omissions result from accident, negligence, or any other cause.

The information contained within this Book is strictly for educational purposes. If you wish to apply ideas contained in this Book, you are taking full responsibility for your actions

Chapter 1. Commercial Real Estate

When I was developing this quick learning guide one of my main priorities was to make it simple, yet concise and with great learning value. I don't want to spend 2 chapters with boring content so let's get down to business.

Now let's start for learning the basics about the Commercial Real Estate industry. For this purpose we will review all important definitions that you will be using several times a day now that you decided to pursue a position and/or career in this awesome line of business.

Important Definitions

Real Estate: is "property consisting of land and the buildings on it, along with its natural resources such as crops, minerals or water; immovable property of this nature; an interest vested in this (also) an item of real property, (more generally) buildings or housing in general. Also: the business of real estate; the profession of buying, selling, or renting land, buildings or housing."[1] It is a legal term used in jurisdictions whose legal system is derived from English common law, such as India, the United Kingdom, United States, Canada, Pakistan, Australia, and New Zealand.

(Source https://en.wikipedia.org/wiki/Real_estate)

There are two kinds of Real Estate properties based on the use they are intended to serve: Residential and Commercial Real Estate.

Residential Real Estate properties can be single family or multifamily structures which should be occupied for non-business purposes only. Keep in mind that ahead we will discuss investment properties or income producing residential properties. These kinds of properties fall in both ends and for the same reason some lenders may consider a duplex as a commercial building when a different lender will consider the same property as a residential multiple unit property as long as this is owner occupied. For some lenders a residential multi-unit property may be considered as commercial if the property holds more than 4 units.

Commercial Real Estate properties are structures which sole intent is to be used for commercial and business purposes. Within this classification there are different types of Commercial CRE that we will revise ahead. Some examples of Commercial CRE are: churches, gas stations, schools, gyms, shopping malls, office buildings, hotels, hospitals, apartment complex and more.

Always take under account that even when the listing shows a property as residential or commercial the lender always decides what classification best fit the subject property. This is an important factor since based on this classification the property may or may not qualify for financing with certain lenders.

Income Producing RE Previously I mentioned income producing real estate properties. These types of real estate are properties bought by an entity or individual to earn income through renting, leasing or price appreciation. Your primary home residence can never be considered as an income producing property even if you lease a portion of your property (basement units for example). Depending on the State where you will be conducting your business activities local laws and regulations may need to be considered while classifying a prospect property as income producing real estate.

Non-income producing properties are those which don't generate rental or leasing income. When you own a commercial property this cannot be considered as income producing since your source of income is the business operating in the property. These are so types of non-income producing properties. Churches, car dealerships, amusement parks, zoos, truck stops, bowling alleys, day care centers, marinas, hospitals, convenience stores, cemeteries/funeral homes, business condos, gas stations, auto repair shops, nursing homes, airports, auto race tracks, casinos, schools, factories, car washes, museums, golf courses and time shares.

So far we have learned different types of Real Estate based on their purpose and ability to generate income. Now we are going to learn about CRE based on the type of tenants occupying the property. There are mainly 2 different types of properties under these criteria: Single Tenant and Multitenant properties.

Single Tenant Properties are solitary free-standing buildings; they must be built on individual parcels of land and always implies a landlord and tenant relationship even if it appears the building is owner occupied. Most Single

Tenant Properties often have long-term leases (10-years+) which makes a great investment opportunity for developers able to secure long term tenants who normally are franchises.

Multiple Tenant

Multitenant Properties are typically occupied by more than one tenant and have shorter leases (2-5 years in general).

Chapter 2. Classification of Commercial Real Estate

Residential Real Estate – Fix & Flipping

A type of real estate in which an investor purchases properties with the goal of making a profit as a result of a hot housing market and/or from renovations and capital improvements.

Residential Real Estate – Rental Property

A type of real estate in which an investor purchases properties with the goal of making a profit as a result of a hot housing market and/or from renovations and capital improvements.

Retail

Retail structure where some form(s) of retail constitutes the sole primary usage. This may include various forms of shops, dining & drinking, and customer-facing service businesses.

Office

Office buildings are used primarily to conduct business (administration, clerical services, consulting, and other client services not related to retail sales) can hold single or multiple firms.

Multifamily

Multifamily (multi-dwelling unit or MDU) multiple separate housing units for residential inhabitants are contained within one building or several buildings within one complex. A common form is an apartment building.

Industrial

Industrial Factories and other premises used for manufacturing, altering, repairing, cleaning, washing, breaking-up, adapting or processing any article; generating power or slaughtering livestock.

Hospitality

Hospitality is a broad category of fields within CRE buildings that includes lodging, event planning and additional fields within the tourism industry

Land

Land intentioned to be used for commercial purposes including building offices, shops, resorts and restaurants as opposed to construction of a residential property.

Special purpose property

Special Purpose Property that is appropriate for one type of use or limited use. This type of property has unique design or layout, uses special construction materials, or other features that limit the property's utility for purposes other than the one for which it was built.

Chapter 3.
Classification of CRE

Commercial Real Estate Classifications

Commercial real estate is categorized into different classes. CRE is divided into four classes: class A, class B, class C or class D.

Class A – Investment grade quality properties with highest rent; nicest, newest and best properties in the best areas; generally owned by institutional investors and less than 10 years old

Class B - Buildings are usually older than and not as good-looking as Class A buildings. These buildings are often targeted by investors for restoration.

Class C - Buildings are the oldest, usually over 20 years of age, located in less attractive areas and in need of maintenance.

Class D – Bad properties in conflicting locations with high rates of crime, legal issues and/or environmental issues

CHAPTER 4.
CRE FINANCE

Loans within the CRE market have registered tremendous growth in the last decade. Many lenders now offer a number of possibilities to finance CRE deal but we will focus on the 4 main streams of CRE financing to help you get a better understanding.

Acquisition loan – used to purchase raw land; high risk, short term loan as collateral value can significantly drop in a recession.

Development loan – used to build the infrastructure on the land (clear, grade, water, sewer, utilities, curb, pavement, etc.) Loan is high risk and short term.

Construction loan – used to build the property; high risk and short term; funded in stages.

Permanent loan – used to pay off the other loans; low risk and long term as payments are based on the stabilized rental income of the property.

Chapter 5. Commercial Real Estate Lenders

Lenders specialized in CRE Finance must be approached based on the particular nature of every deal.

Just because an institutional lender turns down a deal it doesn't mean financing is off the table. When approaching lenders to submit a potential deal, make sure to inquire first about their lending guidelines. Here are the main types of CRE lenders:

Bank – A financial establishment that uses money deposited by customers for investment purpose pays it out when required, makes loans at interest and exchanges currency.

Life Insurance Companies – A business that provides coverage, in the form of compensation resulting from loss, damages, injury, treatment or hardship in exchange for premium payments.

Agency Lender – Agency lending enables customers to maximize the use of their securities through strategic lending. Lenders are in full control of the risk – they are free to select their counterparties and impose tailored credit limits.

Credit Finance Company – an institution engaged in such specialized forms of financing as purchasing accounts receivable, extending credit to retailers and manufacturers, discounting installment contracts, and granting loans with goods as security.

Private Lender – It refers to lending money to a company or individual by a private individual or organization. While banks are traditional sources of financing for real estate, and other purposes, private money is offered by individuals or organizations and may have nontraditional qualifying guidelines.

Chapter 6. Credit Basics

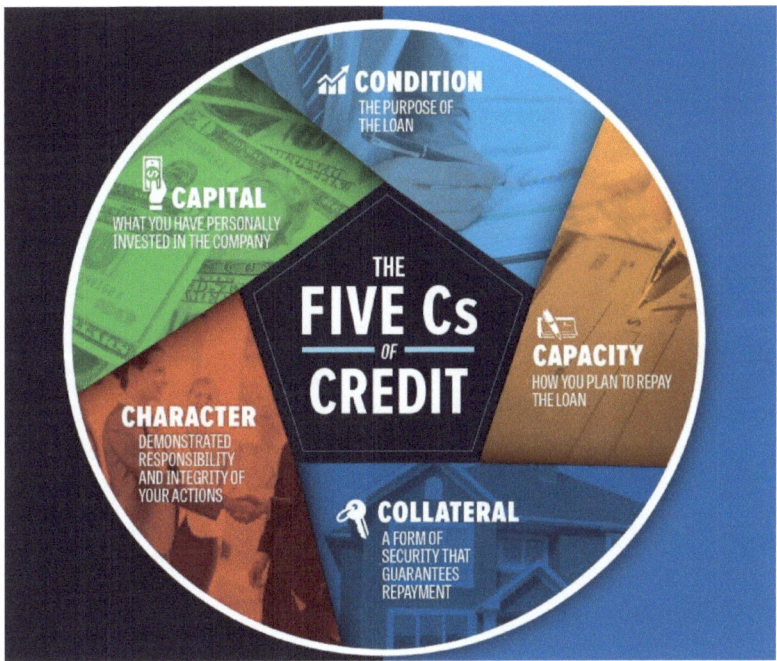

Most CRE deals will require the use of a lender or private investor in order to obtain financing unless is a cash purchase.

Having a general understanding about credit rating will help you maximize your efforts to obtain financing for your next CRE deal.

Let's check the 5 basics of credit rating:

1. Capacity (DSCR) – How much debt can the property handle? Evaluation of the property's history of repayment; Debt Service Coverage Ratio (DSCR or DCR) = Net operating income before debt service / debt service

2. Collateral – CRE loans are secured by the property and the lender has a lien against the property as well as personal guarantees; assignment of rents if default; foreclosure is secondary source of repayment from the sale of the collateral.

3. Character/Credit History – Credit report is a good indication of character. Lenders will look at credit history to determine: Payment behavior and how your potential borrower handles established credit accounts.

4. Capital – How much money is the borrower putting down? We must take under account the equity required to qualify for financing. Remember your main ratio to watch while evaluating equity is LTV (loan to value).

5. Conditions – General analysis of the context around the deal. Be specific and concise while you explain the nature and goals related to your project

Are there environmental risks? Does the borrower have management experience?

Chapter 7. Pre-Qualifying CRE Loans

Loan Summary

Lenders want to know the details about your deal. In many cases underwriters may turn down your deal if the Loan Summary is not concise and compelling. Make sure your Summary covers the following items:

- Property Legal description (Location, sq ft, age, etc.)

- Loan amount requested

- Appraised value

- Project description

- Borrower's history

- Use of loan proceeds

- Exit strategy

- Project Financials
- Conclusions

Loan Purpose

This is where you cover the details about your deal. What is the loan amount requested. How is the borrower planning to use loan proceeds?

Property Legal description

Detailed description of the property's location, sq footage, use of building, year built, meets and bound

Time sensitivity

What is the time frame? When do the borrower needs the funds released?

Exit strategy

The main rule about exit strategies is that there is no golden rule to differentiate between strategies for particular scenarios. Therefore, to determine which real estate exit strategy best fits your project will depend on your knowledge of the following factors:

- Short and long-term goals
- Experience level
- Time to close
- Purchase price
- Terms
- Property value
- Condition of the property
- Market conditions
- Supply and demand
- Financing options
- Profit potential
- Location of the property

Chapter 8. Appraisals and CRE Valuation

Appraisals

Real Estate Valuation

Estimating the value of real property is important to a variety of endeavors, including real estate financing, listing real estate for sale, investment analysis, property insurance and the taxation of real estate.

Value

A main consideration in appraising is to determine a property's value: the present worth of future benefits arising from the ownership of real property. The 4 items of value:

- Demand - the desire or need for ownership supported by the financial means to satisfy the desire

- Utility - the ability to satisfy future owners' desires and needs

- Scarcity - the finite supply of competing properties

- Transferability - the ease with which ownership rights are transferred.

Value vs Cost and Price

Value is not necessarily equal to cost or price. Cost refers to actual expenditures; for example, materials and labor. For instance, if a new owner finds a serious flaw in the property, such as a faulty foundation, the value of the property could be lower than the price.

Market Value

The goal of an appraisal is to determine a property's market value: the most probable price that the property will bring in a competitive and open market.

Market Price

Market price, the price at which a property actually sells, may not always represent the market value.

Appraisal Methods

An accurate appraisal depends on the methodical collection of data. Specific data, covering details regarding the particular property, and general data, pertaining to the nation, region, city and neighborhood wherein the property is located, are collected and analyzed to arrive at a value.

Sales Comparison Approach

It is an estimate of value derived by comparing a property with recently sold properties with similar characteristics. Adjustments: it is an estimate of value derived by comparing a property with recently sold properties with similar characteristics.

Cost Approach

The cost approach can be used to estimate the value of properties that have been improved by one or more buildings Depreciation: For appraisal purposes, depreciation refers to any condition that negatively affects the value of an improvement to real property.

Income Capitalization Approach

This method of real estate valuation, and is based on the relationship between the rate of return an investor requires and the net income that a property produces

ABOUT THE AUTHOR

Isaac Arellano
Senior Underwriter
Commercial and Corporate Finance Specialist

My sixteen + years of work experience in the US as a Senior Underwriter working for Commercial Real Estate Investment Funds, Brokers, Commercial Mortgage Bankers and Private Lenders helped me develop mastery in the CRE Underwriting and Finance.

Former clients have used my underwriting and analysis services to close over US$20 billion worth of debt and equity transactions for development, "value-add" and opportunistic acquisitions.

www.ingramcontent.com/pod-product-compliance
Lightning Source LLC
Chambersburg PA
CBHW040259220526
45473CB00002B/529